OUR EVEREST ADVENTURE

OUR EVEREST ADVENTURE

The pictorial history from Kathmandu to the summit

by JOHN HUNT

1954

Brockhampton Press *LEICESTER*

Brigadier Sir John Hunt, C.B.E., D.S.O.

First published in 1954
by Brockhampton Press Ltd
Market Place, Leicester.
Made in Great Britain.
Engraved and printed by
Rembrandt Photogravure Ltd at Watford.
Bound by Hazell Watson & Viney Ltd at Aylesbury.
Designed by Gerald Wilkinson

FOREWORD

To those who do not climb, it is not easy to describe life and its problems high upon a great Himalayan peak. Even those who have climbed or walked among our European Alps and other ranges of similar scale cannot fully appreciate the gigantic dimensions of these highest of all mountains, nor realize the problems – climatic and technical – peculiar to climbing above 23,000 feet or so.

The written word, however inspired or carefully chosen, is a poor vehicle to carry a scene or event from the memory of the writer to the mind of readers who may have no comparable experience: pictures, too, are a frozen record; they capture a moment of history, but it is silent and still – they lack the live drama of movement and sound. But presented with the two side by side you may, with a little imagination, feel yourself transported to that strange world surrounding Everest and share a few of our experiences as we prepared and then made progress up that mountain.

I had always hoped that we, who lived among those mountains and whose memories will ever bear the imprint of that experience, would be able to share the events of last summer with all those others who wished us well, who waited breathless as the climax drew near. That is what has been attempted in this book. It is primarily a pictorial record, designed to bring to life the story as I attempted to describe it in *The Ascent of Everest*. The words are the same as those I wrote in that book; it is, in fact, a shorter version brought to life by photographs.

But pictures cannot convey what motives prompted a certain action; they cannot justify it nor comment upon its place in history. These thoughts have not been carried into the text of this book. Just in case you are left wondering how and why it all came about, let me explain that we were attempting to solve, in 1953, a problem which had defeated a number of other climbers over a period of 32 years. Most of the previous expeditions were British, but in 1952 two Swiss Expeditions had attempted, in succession, to climb Everest. Until after the last war, all these Expeditions had made their attempts from the North, via Tibet, for the approach through Nepal was closed to them; an altitude of over 28,000 feet was attained on several occasions in those years of struggle between the wars. A changed political situation in 1949-50 made it both possible and necessary to open a new line of attack from the South. It was pioneered by a British party led by Eric Shipton, and the Swiss, following closely on his heels, succeeded in their turn in forcing a route to within about 1,000 feet from the top.

It is against this background that you should read this book, for although many of the problems faced and solved by our predecessors were still great and serious problems to us, we were the wiser for their hard experience and we were given confidence by their achievements.

Finally, you may be wondering why we and all those others strove to climb Everest, and whether all this effort was worth while. These questions are inter-related; if, in answer to the first question, I tell you that it was not to attain fame that we did so, that we set out to solve a great and difficult problem which was a challenge to man's spirit and skill, I feel I have also answered the second question. But not completely, for I shall never feel the ascent of Everest was really worthwhile if it has done no more than win applause. I hope that the moral which may be read in this story of the long drawn-out struggle to reach one of the ends of the earth, will have its effect in shaping the characters and steering the actions of our young people, both now and for generations to come.

I wish to record my appreciation of the fine work of Gerald Wilkinson and Elsie Herron in compiling this book, and to pay again a tribute, both to Alfred Gregory and other members of the Expedition who took the photographs, and also to Messrs. Kodak, Ilford and Agfa, who so generously supplied the film and other photographic material.

John Hunt

Camberley, 24 Feb 1954

CONTENTS

Changtse   North Col   Everest

ingtren   Lho La   Khumbu Icefall

The Times Photograph

Western Cwm

The Reconnaissance Expedition of 1921 had discovered in broad outline the geography of the south-western side of Mount Everest. The three great peaks of the massif, Everest, Lhotse and Nuptse, together with their high connecting ridges, enclosed a basin which Mallory named the West Cwm. (Mallory had climbed a great deal in North Wales and for that reason he used the Welsh spelling of the word 'combe'.) Any approach to the South Col must lie up this hidden valley, which enclosed the whole of the southern aspect of Mount Everest.

ERIC SHIPTON

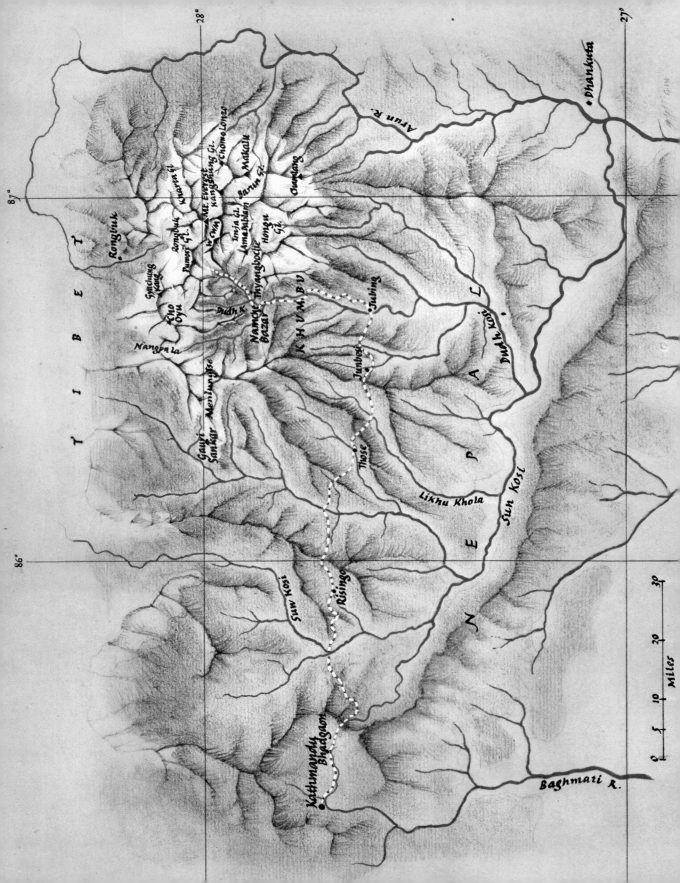

THE MARCH TO KHUMBU

Our various journeys by air, sea, rail and, ultimately, on foot, converged on Kathmandu, the capital city of the Kingdom of Nepal.

On 3rd March, Tom Bourdillon and I flew over the densely wooded foothills of Nepal into the open Valley beyond. As we skimmed low over the final ridge, the high Himalaya could be seen spread out over a great distance, mile upon mile of remote mountains making a crenellated backcloth of dazzling whiteness behind the browns and greens of the intervening ridges. We could see countless peaks between the bastions of Annapurna, the highest mountain yet climbed, and Everest, so soon to be assailed by ourselves.

During the following days, those of us who travelled by air gathered in this fascinating city of Kathmandu, to be joined at the end of the first week of March by the main party. The latter part of their journey had involved long, dusty stages from Bombay in a succession of trains, degenerating into a ride on a lorry perched on top of our mountainous baggage, and finally an eighteen-mile march over the ridges which bar entry into the Valley of Nepal.

India was exceptionally hot for that season – little below 100° F in the shade – and in the heat and dust they had had the anxiety of watching over the transference of 473 packages, weighing seven-and-a-half tons, from ship to train, from large trains to smaller trains, from the miniature Nepal railway to lorries and, finally, from road head in southern Nepal to the conveyor trays of an overhead rope way on the last stage, over the high ridges to Kathmandu. The Nepalese Army most kindly made space for us to instal a baggage depot in their lines at the town of Bhadgaon, eight miles east of Kathmandu, whither we arranged to ferry the loads from the rope way. This would save a whole day's march from the city.

Stobart   *Pugh*   *Noyce*   *Evans*

Band   *Ward*   *Hillary*   *Bourdillon*   *Westmacott*

Gregory   *Lowe*   *Hunt*   *Tenzing*   *Wylie*

Meanwhile, our party was being looked after in delightfully informal comfort by our Ambassador, Christopher Summerhayes, and his staff. We could not have had a better send off.

We had requested the Himalayan Club to select for us twenty of the best Sherpas for work at high altitude and to arrange for their arrival in Kathmandu early in March. The Sherpas are hillmen whose home is in the district of Sola Khumbu in Eastern Nepal. Many of them have migrated to Darjeeling in the Indian State of Bengal where they have made porterage for foreign expeditions their livelihood. Cheerful, loyal and courageous, exceptionally hardy, a few of them have now reached a good standard of proficiency as snow and ice climbers. They are wonderful companions on a mountain.

These were to be the men intended for carrying our loads to the head of the Western Cwm, thence to the South Col; a select band of six from this number were to be earmarked for the Assault parties. They duly arrived on 4th March, and with them was our Sirdar, the already renowned Tenzing. When he became one of our climbing party, he was thirty-nine, and it was his sixth visit to Everest. By virtue of his wonderful exploit with the Swiss guide Lambert in 1952, Tenzing established himself not only as the foremost climber of his race but as a mountaineer of world standing. It was a meeting we had looked forward to with keen anticipation. We were soon firm friends.

The Sherpas from Darjeeling made a colourful sight that morning as they paraded for our inspection. Most of them wore an assortment of garments which they had obtained on previous expeditions – green berets, blue ski-ing caps, balaclavas, bright-coloured sweaters and outsize boots. Some of these Sherpas were already known to us and had been specially asked for: Thondup, the cook, the two brothers Da Tensing and Annullu. Then there was the solemn, enigmatic Ang Namgyal and his near namesake Da Namgyal, who had done illustrious service with the Swiss in the spring and autumn of 1952, and the big, jocular Pasang Phutar II. These and several others came forward, grinning shyly, to be introduced to us in the Embassy garden. Accompanying the Sherpas were a number of Sherpanis, their wives and sweethearts,

Da Tensing

Annullu

Da Namgyal

Ang Nyima

who hoped to be engaged as coolies on our journey to their native land. I was delighted to agree, for not only would they add colour and gaiety to our company, but they carry loads as stoutly as their menfolk.

March 9th was a day of tremendous activity at Bhadgaon, with the baggage party, consisting of Charles Evans and Wilfrid Noyce, sorting and arranging the packages, opening those containing our requirements in clothing and equipment for the march and directing the work of others.

Charles Wylie was now faced with the difficult task of engaging a small army of coolies to carry the baggage on the seventeen-day journey to Thyangboche, a monastery which we had chosen from a study of the map as our first Base Camp, and from which we could carry out our initial programme of training. Coincident with the dumping of the loads on the parade ground at Bhadgaon, Charles mustered some three hundred and fifty local men to shoulder their burdens. The loads proved so numerous that I decided to move off in two caravans at an interval of twenty-four hours. The track along which we should be moving allows only for single-line foot traffic as it enters more rugged country, and only by shortening our "tail" could we avoid a very protracted departure from one stage and arrival at the next.

In addition to these hectic activities, there were also social occasions. We were most kindly entertained by the King of Nepal and by the Indian Ambassador; a charming reception was organized at the British Embassy in our honour.

March 10th was the date for the departure of the first caravan. I intended to stay in order to ensure that the second party got away without any last-minute hitches, after which I would go forward covering two stages in one day and catch up the leaders. All of us went out to Bhadgaon to see them off; it was a memorable occasion, and there was an upsurge of excitement in the air, as many hundreds of men hurried hither and thither, chattering as they tied and adjusted their burdens. Moving among them were Charles Wylie and Tenzing. There was an atmosphere of complete order despite the large-scale movement which was about to begin; Charles and Tenzing had done a magnificent job in getting us away to this encouragingly well-organized start. Pressmen and other onlookers had come to see us off and there was much clicking of cameras as the long stream of coolies started off into the town on their way eastwards.

Later that morning, I returned to the Embassy with three members of the party who were to travel with the second caravan. I heaved yet another of many sighs of relief; at last we were on the final stage of our approach to the mountain.

In London I had fretted mentally at the prospect of having to spend nearly three weeks before we should be able to get to grips with the more serious part of the programme. Now, with seventeen days' journey ahead of us, the feeling of urgency was dispelled by the simple beauty of the countryside, by the removal, for a time, of worry and the exasperation of paperwork. Our programme was carefully timed and we knew there was no advantage in forcing the pace, even had this been practicable; we could appreciate the scenery to the full, indulge our own particular interests and enjoy the company of one another.

Our track led us eastwards, thus cutting across the natural lines of drainage from the Himalayan watershed. We were moving athwart the grain of the land – down into deep valleys, across foaming torrents or broader, swift-flowing rivers and up the far hillsides. This was big country, with long views across broad expanses of mountainside, vast, fertile and dotted with friendly cottages. Along the track we passed plenty of local folk, the girls colourful in their big ear-rings, glass bangles and red bead necklaces, the men close-cropped, drably and very scantily attired to suit the climate. On the dividing ridges we entered the lovely

rhododendron belt, gnarled trees whose blossoms graduated with increasing height from scarlet to pink, and above 10,000 feet, to white and yellow. The forests were besprinkled with white magnolia flowers, heavily scented, fallen from the trees. Mauve primulas bedecked the path and Himalayan bird life was a constant source of wonder.

16

As we went further east, the views of the bigger peaks became more magnificent. I remember how, on the fifth day's march, we had climbed steadily up to a pass at about 8,000 feet, there to be confronted with a stupendous view to the north. The great group of Gauri Sankar peaks, the highest of them, Menlungtse, over 23,000 feet, were startlingly close and fascinating in their abruptness. As we went further east, the views of the bigger peaks became more magnificent, less unreal.

We followed a leisurely routine. We would rise at 5.30 a.m. with the aid of a cup of tea. The whole caravan would be on the move soon after 6 a.m. Our kitchen staff would go ahead, with Thondup in the lead, to select a suitable place for breakfast. Arriving at some delectable stream after two to three hours, we would make a prolonged halt, and while the cook made his fire and prepared porridge, bacon and eggs, we would swim and rest, some reading or writing, others watching birds, catching butterflies and insects. Camp would be reached in the early afternoon.

These walks between stages and our leisure hours in camp worked wonders in our relationship. Favourable first impressions warmed into firm friendships;

we quickly learned to appreciate one another. At the same time we also made friends with our Sherpas.

I began to be preoccupied again with plans and spent hours with Ed Hillary and Charles Evans talking over alternative methods of assault and calculating their implication in terms of loads. At other times I was able to relax and observe my companions as we lay in our big Dome tent.

There was usually a small group – it might be Michael Westmacott, George Band and Tom Bourdillon – exchanging views on some ultra-severe rock climb. Tom Stobart would be recounting some thrilling if slightly improbable experience with wild game in Africa, or giving a vivid description of the Far South. George Lowe might be speaking in serious mood about one of his many experiences and interests, not least among them the apparently unequal struggle between the unfortunate teachers in New Zealand and their unruly and enterprising pupils; or he might be competing with the sparkling wit of George Band, to make us ache with laughter in his guise of expedition clown. In contrast to the remainder, Gregory would be quietly reading or talking abstruse photographic technicalities with Stobart; Wilf Noyce, no less unobtrusive, would be scribbling page upon

At rest on the march

page of closely-written manuscript in one of his large notebooks. Of course, at frequent intervals there arose the ever-fascinating if controversial topic of food. This would arouse even Greg from his corner and provide Ed Hillary with his favourite topic. And into any of these groups we might hear a quiet intervention from Charles Evans, rounding off a jest or adding information to some discussion from his wide knowledge, always sound and sensible. They were a grand crowd.

About half-way along the route, Ed Hillary, Tenzing and I remained behind for a day to see the second party. It was good to find them, like ourselves, in fine form. They had had a few excitements: the visit of a panther to their camp one night, a fight with 'kukris' – local knives – between a Sherpa and a coolie. And there had been sacrifices to science which I was glad to have avoided. Griff Pugh had subjected the party to a fearful ordeal known as a 'maximum work test,' consisting of rushing uphill at best possible speed until the lungs were bursting and then expiring air into an enormous bag until it swelled out like a balloon. We hurried forward to catch up the others lest we should be tested in our turn.

On the ninth day of our march we crossed a pass at 9,000 feet and entered the district of Sola Khumbu. The mountainsides became more precipitous and rugged, cultivation was patchy and cottages more scattered; the scenery became first more Alpine and then more truly Himalayan. Equally marked was the changed appearance of the people. We recognized the pronounced Mongolian features, broad and bland; the heavier, more decorative clothing. This was Sherpaland.

So far we had been moving steadily eastwards; now, shortly after crossing a last ridge, the highest of all – nearly 12,000 feet – we found our track leading us down, down to the deep gorge of the Dudh Kosi. This was the turning point of our journey, for after crossing the river by an unstable temporary structure of bamboos, boulders and turf, we swung northwards up the east flank of the gorge, heading straight towards our final destination. The views, whether down the plunging slopes to the distant river, or skywards to the jagged crest of the enclosing ridges above which peeped the icy pinnacles of Everest's near neighbours, were alike breathtaking.

As we advanced up the valley, we could see the huge buttress of open, grassy hillsides at which the Dudh Kosi is joined by a notable tributary, the Bhote Kosi. The Dudh Kosi, carrying the waters of melted ice from a wide arena of mountain country to the west of Everest, was the one we were to follow, but first we must climb the buttress dividing the two rivers to reach Namche Bazar, the chief village of Khumbu.

The last bridge; over the Dudh Kosi

Looking up the Imja Khola to Everest. Thyangboche is below the ridge in the centre

We went up the broad path to Namche on 25th March. Many people were on the move, gay and bright-coloured folk. It was a grand, clear morning, and we climbed for a time aside from the track in order to see the view up the Imja Khola. Suddenly, there was what we had been waiting for – Everest, now real in its nearness, its solid pyramid soaring above the long snow-fringed arete joining Lhotse and Nuptse.

Just before entering the village, we were greeted by a small deputation, relatives of our men, waiting by the path with a barrel of milky-coloured *chang*, a beer brewed from rice, and a large teapot of Tibetan tea, its spout and handle decorated with coloured paper. This delightful welcome, mainly for the Sherpas but also for ourselves, is typical of these friendly people.

The final day of the march was also the climax to the mounting pleasure – indeed, the thrills – which we had been experiencing since the day we left the Valley of Nepal. Thyangboche must be one of the most beautiful places in the world. The height is well over 12,000 feet. The Monastery buildings stand upon a knoll. Surrounded by satellite dwellings, all quaintly constructed and oddly mediaeval in appearance, it provides a grandstand beyond comparison for the finest mountain scenery that I have ever seen. Beyond a foreground of dark firs, lichen-draped birch and dwarf rhododendrons, tower immense ice peaks in every quarter. The Everest group bars the head of the valley, the 25,000-foot wall of Nuptse falling in sheer precipice some 7,000 feet from the summit ridge to the glaciers flowing at its base.

We stood, spellbound by this wonderful scene, upon an open grassy alp on which yaks were grazing peacefully – an ideal spot for our first Base Camp. Life was very good.

March 27th Our Base Camp at Thyangboche was a colourful and active
scene during the three days following our arrival there. The
period between the end of the march out and the beginning
of 'acclimatization' was intended to be restful, but we had very
little leisure; there was so much to arrange and plan, and it
was important on no account to encroach on the many other
activities leading up to the target date of readiness to climb the
mountain: May 15th.

John Hunt – *Leader of the Expedition. Aged 42, educated Marlborough and Sandhurst. Commissioned K.R.R.C., 1930. During the war served as Chief Instructor Commando Mountain and Snow Warfare School; then Egypt, Italy and Greece, commanding infantry brigade 4th Indian Division. Recently on staff of S.H.A.P.E. Ten Alpine summer seasons, much rock climbing in Britain. Stationed in India between the wars, had taken part in three Himalayan expeditions.*

Charles Evans, F.R.C.S. – *Aged 33, short and sturdy, sandy-haired; "Quartermaster" and deputy leader of the Expedition. Educated at Shrewsbury; during the war served in the Far East. Climbed with Tilman on the Annapurna range, 1950; in the mountains of Kulu, 1951, with Shipton on Cho Oyu, 1952.*

Edmund Hillary – *Aged 33. A bee-keeper near Auckland, New Zealand; war-service with R.N.Z.A.F. Quickly rose to the foremost rank among New Zealand mountaineers. Took part in both the Reconnaissance and Cho Oyu expeditions; Shipton prophesied he would be a very strong contender for an Everest summit party. Lanky build, abounding in restless energy.*

Bhotia Tenzing Norkey – *Aged 39, a Sherpa born on the borders of Nepal and Tibet, and lives in Darjeeling with his wife and three daughters. Has joined the ranks of nearly every Everest Expedition since 1935. In 1952, with the Swiss guide Lambert, he reached within 1,000 feet of the top of Everest; this achievement established him as a mountaineer of world standing. A Sirdar of unequalled authority with the Sherpas.*

Tom Bourdillon – *Aged 28, accompanied Shipton on both the Reconnaissance and Cho Oyu. Elder son of Dr. R. B. Bourdillon. Educated Gresham's and Oxford; war service in Greece and Egypt. Employed as physicist, Ministry of Supply. Huge and hefty; an outstanding rock climber. In charge of the Expedition's oxygen equipment.*

Alfred Gregory – *Director of a Travel Agency. Climbing mainly in Lake District and Alps, but took part in the Cho Oyu expedition. At 39, the oldest member of the party, apart from the leader; small, wiry and very tough. Expedition photographer.*

George Lowe – *Tall, well-built, aged 28, a teacher at Hastings, New Zealand. Introduced Hillary to some of the high standard climbs in the New Zealand mountains. Lowe was another of Shipton's strong team on Cho Oyu; his ice technique is of very high standard.*

Wilfrid Noyce – *Schoolmaster and author, aged 34, with a fine record of difficult routes in the Alps and on British crags. Had climbed in Garhwal and made an ascent of Pauhunri in Sikkim. The mountaineering equipment of the expedition was his special charge.*

Michael Westmacott – *Aged 27, employed on statistical investigation at Rothamsted Experimental Station. Ex-President of the Oxford University Mountaineering Club. Rock climbing in Britain and four seasons in the Alps. Special responsibility on the expedition for structural equipment and tents.*

Charles Wylie – *Aged 32, a serving officer of the Brigade of Gurkhas. Educated Marlborough and Sandhurst. P.o.W. in Malaya and Siam, 1942-45. Has climbed regularly since boyhood in Britain, Alps and Himalaya. Organizing secretary and transport officer of the 1953 Expedition.*

Dr. Michael Ward – *Aged 28, educated Marlborough, Cambridge and London Hospital; served R.A.M.C. 1950-52. Suggested and took part in the Reconnaissance of Everest from the South side in 1951. A most useful climbing reserve, but primarily Expedition doctor.*

George Band – *Aged 23; tall, bespectacled, studious, the youngest of the party. Specialized in geology at Cambridge; ex-President of that University's Mountaineering Club. Has climbed in Britain and the Alps since 1948. In charge of the Expedition's wireless equipment and, with Griffith Pugh, food.*

Griffith Pugh – *Aged 43. Physiologist sponsored by the Medical Research Council. Had done valuable physiological work during the Cho Oyu Expedition. Long-distance skier – Oxford, British Universities and Olympic (1936) teams. Joined Medical Research Council in 1950.*

Tom Stobart – *Aged 35. Photographer taking film for Countryman Films. Photographer on Norwegian-British-Swedish Antarctic Expedition 1949-52. Has climbed in Alps, Carpathians and Himalaya.*

Evans and
Hillary after
the ascent

Wylie
at Base Camp

Lowe
on the South Col

Pugh

Tenzing and
a friend at
Thyangboche

Bourdillon

Westmacott

Stobart

Gregory

Noyce
at Camp IV

Ward
at Base Camp

Band
at Thyangboche

After breakfast – Hunt and Ward

For the first time, we have pitched all our tents, about twenty of them of various shapes, sizes and colours: three miniature ones intended for a final camp; orange ones for Advance Base and above; yellow ones of a similar pattern to be used as far as the entrance to the Western Cwm; a distinctive Swiss tent which is Tenzing's temporary home, and two bigger dome-shaped tents, one used by the Sherpas and the other by ourselves. In one far corner of the compound, Thondup has set up his cookhouse. Among his many minions are the Sherpanis, who are busy, some cleaning cooking-pots or mending garments, others combing and plaiting each other's long black tresses. We ourselves have finished a leisurely breakfast, seated on packing-cases around a table improvised from Tom Bourdillon's oxygen boxes.

Band demonstrates the portable radio to Hunt

Now the day's work is in progress in earnest and there are a number of little groups engaged on different jobs. To some, Tom Bourdillon, with Mike Ward to help him, is giving a lesson in the Open-Circuit oxygen. Ed Hillary is the centre of another party, mostly composed of Sherpas, as he demonstrates Cooke's specially adapted Primus stove. George Band is unpacking the portable wireless sets.

Ama Dablam; telephoto from Thyangboche

REHEARSALS

We now had a period of about three weeks – until 20th April – in which to train and prepare ourselves for Everest. The main purpose of this period was to get used gradually to increasing height – to acclimatize – and we also planned to practise with both types of oxygen apparatus and get used to other equipment. The programme was to be carried out in two halves, each of about eight days.

We divided ourselves into three parties, which would be looked after by Ed Hillary, Charles Evans and myself. Different areas were chosen for each party.

Charles's group was the first to leave, on 29th March. They were to use both the Closed- and Open-Circuit apparatus and had therefore a particularly full programme. The rest of us were to start off the following day, and all were to return to Base by 6th April.

By then we had all succeeded in climbing to the maximum height attainable in that early season and had done so without distress. It is unlikely that peaks of

20,000 feet have ever been climbed at this time of year. There was unmistakable confidence in the oxygen equipment, both in its design and its effects. Morale was evidently high. Most satisfactory of all was to observe how our friendship and confidence in each other had increased. There was an atmosphere of relaxation and simple happiness which gave me assurance of our combined strength when the testing time should come.

Our second stay at Thyangboche seemed to be even busier than the first. About a fortnight would elapse before the whole party would gather together again. This meeting would be at the new Base Camp, to be sited as high as practicable up the Khumbu glacier.

Earlier planning had given too little importance to the Khumbu Icefall. Our discussions left me in no doubt that more time must be given to a thorough reconnaissance of this and to the preparation of a route up it, if we were not to lose precious days later. One party was therefore composed for this task in the second acclimatization period. It consisted of Ed Hillary, whose previous knowledge of the Icefall would be invaluable; George Lowe, by virtue of his outstanding ice-craft; George Band and Michael Westmacott, the latter especially because of his responsibility for the structural equipment, which was expected to be required on this section of the route.

Then there was the need to instruct an élite band of Sherpas in the use of oxygen. This had not been attempted before, but it formed an important part of

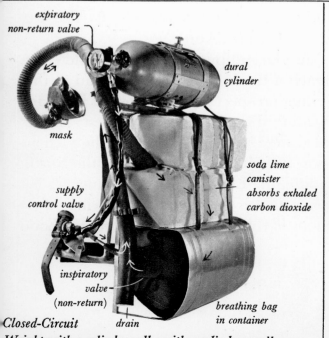

expiratory non-return valve

mask

supply control valve

inspiratory valve (non-return)

drain

dural cylinder

soda lime canister absorbs exhaled carbon dioxide

breathing bag in container

Closed-Circuit
Weight with 1 cylinder 35lb, with 2 cylinders 47 lb

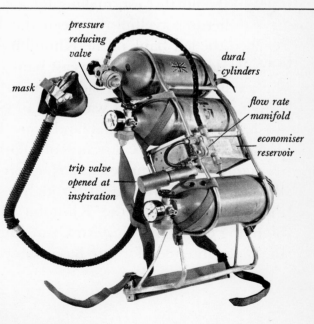

pressure reducing valve

mask

trip valve opened at inspiration

dural cylinders

flow rate manifold

economiser reservoir

Open-Circuit
Weight with 3 cylinders 41lb, with 1 cylinder 18 lb

the plan that six or more of these men should be able to climb above the South Col with the summit parties. Oxygen would immeasurably increase the chances of their doing so. In order to combine this task of instruction with that of closing our present Base, linking up with the oxygen convoy now approaching under Jimmy Roberts, 'signing up' our Low Altitude Sherpas and bringing all our remaining gear up to the new site, I requested Charles Wylie, Charles Evans, Gregory and Tenzing to cut short their training period and return to Thyangboche to fulfil this last assignment.

My own party, this time consisting of Michael Ward, Tom Bourdillon and Wilfrid Noyce, was to join the Icefall team at the end of this period, which was due to be completed by 17th April.

On 9th April we left Charles Evans's party at Dingboche, a village at a height of just under 15,000 feet below the sheer north-west face of Ama Dablam. Here he would carry out his indoctrination of the Sherpas in the mysteries of oxygen. There had been some doubts about the prospects of giving them confidence in this strange auxiliary to uphill movement, but it proved a great success.

My party decided to carry on up the valley. We eventually camped at about 16,500 feet, beneath the north ridge of Ama Dablam. After three days, during which we trained the Sherpas in ice work among the séracs of a wide arena of glaciers flowing from a fine ridge on the opposite side of the combe in which we were camping, the party descended to the valley. Crossing it, we climbed the hill-sides to the north-west, making for a col which was known to be used in summer by yak-herds travelling between the Imja and Khumbu pastures. By this we reached the left bank of the Khumbu glacier on 14th April.

Next day we followed the east bank of the glacier upwards until we could cross the ice-stream to the far side so as to reach a track leading to the head of the valley. It was a glorious walk and an exciting prospect lay before us. At long last we had turned the corner and were heading directly towards Everest. As we dodged between the wilderness of colossal granite boulders bestrewing the glacier, we sighted a peak made famous by pre-war expeditions: Changtse, or the North Peak of Everest. We saw it through a saddle, the Lho La, which we knew to be the point at which the Khumbu glacier makes its sensational swing after plunging out of the Western Cwm; the foot of this gap must therefore be about the place intended for our Base Camp.

An air of expectancy remained with us all that day. By early afternoon, we had reached a shallow glacial lake between the moraine and the mountainside beneath the southern rampart of Pumori, where the Swiss had made their Base Camp last spring; stone circles or 'sangars,' evidently served as windbreaks for their tents. This, Lake Camp, was to be our resting-place until we moved up to join Ed's party for work on the Icefall.

April 9th Hillary's party for the second acclimatization period was much larger than Charles's or mine. He had with him Pugh and Stobart with their considerable specialized baggage, in addition to the equipment required to prepare a route up the Icefall as far as the Western Cwm. Moreover, he would have to be self-contained in rations until the last party came up from Thyangboche on 22nd April. He must also have food for my party when we joined him. To carry his loads he had thirty-nine coolies and five Sherpas, making his party fifty in all.

Soon after leaving us, he ran into a bad spell of weather. Snow had not been expected before he reached his destination, and we had not thought it necessary to provide his coolies with special equipment, such as boots and goggles. Ploughing on in their felt boots through the heavy snow, his caravan arrived in a very wretched condition at the end of the second day; cold, wet and with many cases of snow-blindness.

They were short of tents and though a surprising number of the party, which included a good many women, squeezed into the available shelters, others had to sleep out in the snow. But these Khumbu folk are tough and proud of it. All but a few, and those the worst affected by snow blindness, were cheerfully ready to start next morning. Ed Hillary and his party improvised protection for the eyes from black tape and pieces of coloured celluloid.

April 11th Passing the Lake Camp, they continued up-glacier, following a line of cairns built by the Swiss last year, along a broad, stony avenue in the centre of the ice, hemmed in by a strange forest of miniature ice peaks on either hand.

It was an odd, unreal landscape, not without a certain beauty. But we were now launched into an unfriendly, dead world, its attractions those of a lunar landscape, for after leaving the moraine above Lake Camp no grass grows, nothing lives.

35

The site of Base Camp, looking towards Lingtren

Close under Lho La, but at a safe distance from the tell-tale fan of pulverized ice and rock avalanche debris at its foot, they found the remnants of the Swiss Camp I. The site was not an ideal one, but it had the important advantage of being close to the foot of the great Icefall; they had only to climb a minor ice-hill behind the tents in order to enjoy a full view of their problem.

Nearing the foot of the Icefall. Ice pinnacles

Ice needles at Base Camp

Base Camp was established on 12th April. The Icefall reconnaissance party were ready to set about their important task.

A later picture of Base Camp, after snow. Looking down-glacier

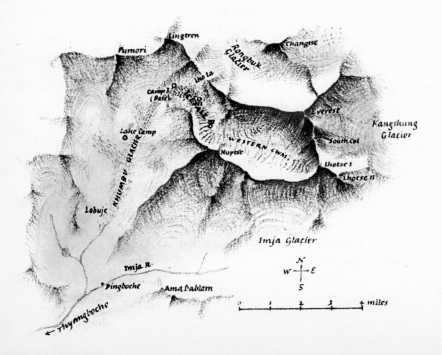

THE ICEFALL

An icefall is a frozen cascade of ice, often on a gigantic scale.
The Khumbu icefall is indeed a monster of the species. Moving
over a steep underlying bed of rock, the surface of the glacier
becomes split into a maze of chasms, tottering and fallen blocks
of ice. Despite the fact that it had been forced by Shipton's
party in 1951 and twice by the Swiss last year, here was a serious
obstacle, whose character could be expected to have changed
beyond recognition by the time we reached it.

Let me show you this staircase leading to the first floor of the
great mansion that is Everest as we saw it. Squeezed between
the shoulders of Everest and Nuptse, the ice resembles a
gigantic cascade, pouring in leaping waves and eddies towards
us. Almost, you might expect to hear the roar of that immense
volume of foaming water which is plunging down with terri-
fying power. But it has been gripped by the cold, frozen into
immobility, a silent thing, its force restrained. But not quite.
For this labyrinth of broken ice is moving, its surface changing,
if not at the pace of water, at least at a speed which makes it
a perilous problem to surmount.

Viewed with the eye of a climber, the problem falls naturally
into two parts. There is a steep lower section, on which there
has obviously been some fairly recent and major change in the
ice, for over a considerable area it has been shattered into a
maze of monstrous ice boulders. At the top of this huge step, at
least 1,000 feet high, there is a shelf where the general angle
lies back briefly before rising again to the lip of the Western
Cwm. This upper section is very foreshortened and partly
hidden by the lower step, but it gives, even from here, the
impression of being less broken up, the lines of cleavage
clearer-cut and on a bigger scale. On both sides of the Icefall
are troughs, which in themselves might give passable routes,
but so menaced are both by the ice avalanches from the
enclosing ridges that to use them would be suicidal. A way
must be found roughly up the middle, through the area where
the ice is most disfigured and chaotic.

40

The lower part of the Icefall rising 1,400 feet to the site of Camp II

Westmacott and Ward setting out to find a route up the Icefall and mark it with flags

Ward cutting steps

April 13th The Icefall party set to work under considerable difficulties. Immediately on arrival, George Lowe fell sick; their strength was further weakened a few days later, when Michael Westmacott was stricken. Although never reduced below an effective strength of three at any one time, this threw an additional strain on the party and their already arduous work was made more difficult by the weather. We were now in the season of daily afternoon snowfall; each morning it was necessary to remake the track prepared so laboriously the day before.

43

Lowe in the Icefall

April 16th   Casting to right and left, making numerous false starts and spending many hours each day in the exhausting labour of hacking away masses of ice, cutting staircases of steps safe for the laden Sherpas, they eventually won through on 16th April and set up two tents at 19,400 feet. Camp II, so hardly won, possessed in those early days a glamour which it was quickly to lose, thanks to familiarity, the dirt from many parties in transit and the increasing heat. Ed Hillary, Lowe and Band spent the night there and next day went to reconnoitre a route up to the edge of the Western Cwm.

Camp II with Pumori

April 17th I left our resting-place at Lake Camp to learn their news and, finding at Base Camp that they were up the Icefall, asked Ang Namgyal to join me in a journey to Camp II. I did not realize at that time that this silent, poker-faced little man had been going up and down this rickety and dangerous route for the past three days; he got ready without a word. Tom Stobart came along with us for some part of the way and pointed out several of the landmarks.

Fixing crampons

It should be remembered that the route, at that time, was not yet ready for use as a highway by laden men. For over half an hour we threaded our way along a series of twisting, narrow ice channels between pinnacles, heading generally towards the foot of the Icefall, but making many detours to avoid obstacles. At last the ice steepened and it became necessary to put on crampons and rope up. This place was named 'The Island'.

'*Mike's Horror*'

Some distance above us, a staircase had been cut up the steep edge of a large crevasse, down which a fixed rope was hanging. Nicknamed "Mike's Horror" after Westmacott, who had led and prepared it, this pitch, now straightforward, told of a fine feat of icemanship. There followed a number of strides over crevasses, two of them too wide to step or jump across.

The crossing of one gap, spanned by two 6-foot sections, demanded a crawling technique, for it was awkward to step upright on the narrow rungs with our spiked boots. Then a steep rise led to the biggest chasm we had yet encountered. A huge block of ice lay wedged across it, abutting against a short wall of ice: the upper lip of the crevasse. Conscious of the aching void below us on our right, we stepped gingerly up a diagonal line of steps. This was 'Hillary's Horror'.

It was a relief to move right, at the top of the shattered section of steepest ice known as 'Hellfire Alley', towards more open ground. We were now in territory which, though carved in larger blocks, was in more active movement, constant and audible.

50

Camp II. The large block of ice at left was a constant menace to climbers

No day passed without some striking change occurring, calling for a fresh reconnaissance of the route into the plateau where our tents of Camp II were pitched. The shelves of ice between cracks were subsiding, making big steps. In time the movement became more violent, the changes more significant. Their sound could be heard from the Camp – a dull, ominous 'wumph' – fortunately they seemed usually to occur at night. It was about 12.30 p.m. when Ang Namgyal and I reached Camp II. Above the tents, we met Hillary, Lowe and Band descending. They had reached the top of the Icefall. This was indeed great news.

After a successful training period and three very full days at Thyangboche, Charles Evans's party were ready to start off for the new Base Camp, moving in two convoys on 18th and 19th April. I went down to meet Charles at Lobuje, one stage below our Lake Camp. With him were Greg and a newcomer to the party, James Morris of *The Times*. While these rear parties approached Base Camp, which Wilfrid Noyce and Mike Ward had gone ahead to re-site some hundreds of yards down the stony avenue in the centre of the glacier, my party moved up from Lake Camp to join Hillary.

Morris

We at once started our task of improving the route up the Icefall, continuing the splendid work of the Reconnaissance party, now having a well-earned rest at Lake Camp. Reinforced by Mike Westmacott, Wilfrid Noyce and Mike Ward, later joined by myself, spent two days between Base and Camp II, cutting many new steps, preparing a safer deviation to avoid 'Hillary's Horror,' fixing new ropes at this and other places.

On 21st April, Mike Westmacott and I remained at Camp II for the night before moving up to the top of the Icefall to choose a site and set up the first tents of Camp III. Next morning we set out, Hillary and Band going ahead to remake and flag the track while Mike Westmacott and I escorted the heavily-laden Sherpas at a slower pace.

Lake Camp

April 22nd I was intrigued to see this upper section of the Icefall for the first time. Here we were moving through ice blocks of bigger dimensions. From the tents of Camp II, the line taken led us for some distance through a gully at the head of the small plateau, then swung steeply up to the right to reach a sérac some 250 feet above the camp. We had to get on to a square-topped section of ice cliff leaning out from the mountainside.

53

A little farther on there was a huge trough at least sixty feet wide, partly filled with chunks of bare ice, and with a narrow platform some twenty feet down, which had sunk from the level of the terrace on which we stood. Here again a staircase had been cut; we added a fixed rope to make the descent more easy. The exit was perhaps the most dangerous part of the whole journey between Base Camp and the Cwm, for the steep slope on the far side of this trough was covered by blocks of ice of all sizes, extending over some 200 feet up the slope. The collapse of any one of these would have spelt disaster to a party below. Three days later, the crevasse had widened by at least a foot. By then we had available logs sent up from Thyangboche, and we improvised a single log 'bridge' and handline, later to be replaced by two sections of the metal ladder. A week after this, this 12-foot ladder was in danger of falling into the chasm.

After turning left in the direction of the Cwm, the only line was to continue along the crest of the débris from the collapse of the cliffs until at last it was possible to reach the foot of the first really solid line of cliffs at the very brink of the Western Cwm, where it spills into the Icefall.

The cliff rises forty feet sheer, so we contoured round its base to the right, passing between the main 'berg' and a large block about twenty feet high. This passage, which we named 'the Nutcracker', was particularly unpleasant both on account of the peculiarly shaky condition of all the ground at the top of the Icefall and the ever-present possibility of another slice peeling off the cliff. There was evidently a hollow space of unknown depth beneath it. Ice fragments falling into the dark abyss set up a prolonged rumbling noise and tremors of the surface, as if an underground train were passing beneath our feet. It was an eerie and frightening sensation.

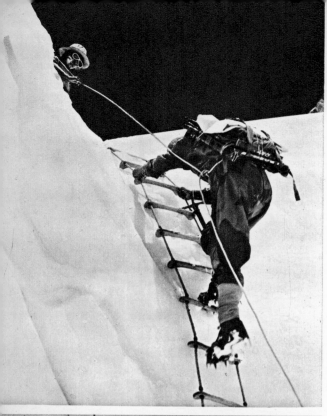

Round the corner the cliff line continued unrelenting, as though to force the intruder right under the fire of avalanches from Nuptse. But there was one weakness in the ice: a narrow, sloping shelf leading to a vertical crack. This crack, which showed where a huge mass would later become detached from the Cwm ice, had been brilliantly led by Hillary on his reconnaissance. Already it was noticeably wider, but aided by the steps he had cut we found much less trouble than he in wriggling up the fifteen feet until our heads appeared suddenly and dramatically on to the level shelf above. This was the highest point reached so far, but it was too near the unreliable edge to make a safe site for Camp III. Rather than bring our Sherpas farther, we hauled the loads up the cliff ourselves at a lower point and went on ourselves, together with Ang Namgyal, to find a good spot. Later Hillary put a rope ladder down the cliff so that loads could be brought up avoiding the ice crack.

The first tent at Camp III. The Lhotse face (centre) is three miles away

The plateau we had reached was itself slowly toppling over the edge, but crossing the more durable of two snow bridges which still spanned the wide crack, we found a shallow scoop not immediately overlooked by other cliffs. It would do admirably for Camp III. The height was about 20,200 feet.

Base Camp

Leaving Hillary, Westmacott and Da Namgyal to improve the route up the upper part of the Icefall, I returned to Base on 22nd April with George Band. Both the rear parties had now arrived and the place was a hive of activity, with a tent perched on each available level space. One of the tree-trunks ordered by Westmacott had been set up as a flagpole for our large Union Jack. As usual, Thondup was efficiently established in a large stone-built kitchen, paved with cardboard from empty ration boxes.

A novel feature was a capacious ice cave tunnelled into one of the big pinnacles behind the tents. It was Tom Stobart's idea for alternative living quarters, and a good one. Base seemed a well-organized and thorough-going concern. Roberts had come up to wish us luck. He had done an inestimable service in delivering us the oxygen consignment by the date required.

58

The only picture of Roberts, unfortunately a back view. With him are Noyce, Wylie and Annullu

One of the first people who came forward as we approached the tents was a small, slightly-built figure with a wizened face and stubbly grey hair. He looked old, but his grin was youthful. It was Dawa Thondup. He had taken part in Himalayan expeditions since 1933.

Dawa and I were very old friends. I had last seen him in 1940 and had specially asked the Himalayan Club to persuade him to join us this year. Thus enlisted, partly for reasons of friendship and sentiment, we could not guess what splendid service this little man was to perform on Everest.

Evans is cutting Lowe's hair. Below, Band and Lowe skinning a yak

Base Camp was not a beautiful place, but it was a haven of luxury to the weary climber. There was good food from Thondup's skilled hands – even fresh beef from a yak slaughtered by Lowe; there was usually a choice of accommodation, whether a Meade tent to yourself, the convivial atmosphere of the Mess tent or the constant temperature of an ice cave. Above all, there was a chance to rest and relax; to sleep, write or read; listen to Radio Ceylon.

Evans and Morris at Lobuje

None the less, the chosen holiday camp was Lobuje, a delectable spot barely two and a half hours' journey from Base Camp. The place consists of a couple of yak-herds' shelters upon a small mound; a spring of fresh, clear water bubbles out strongly from the turf. The earliest flowers were beginning to blossom in early May. Bird and animal life were a delight after living for a time in a dead world. From 2nd May until about the 12th, there was a small but continuous population at Lobuje. One and all benefited enormously both in physical health and renewed zest for the tasks ahead.

THE WESTERN CWM

The hidden valley of the Western Cwm is a wonder of mountain architecture – a high-level glen whose floor slopes gently from about 22,000 feet to 19,000 feet in a westerly direction. At its head stands the great rock peak of Lhotse, 27,000 feet, whose west face falls steeply to the head of the valley, effectively blocking the upper exit. Looking up the Western Cwm, Everest is on the left, its west ridge forming the north enclosing wall. On the opposite side is Nuptse, a ridge rather than a mountain, whose sharp and jagged crest runs for over two miles at a constant elevation of over 25,000 feet. Thus contained between Everest and Nuptse, barred by the face of Lhotse, this astonishing freak of nature leads the climber to the very foot of the mountain; it is the focal point of ascent from the south. On 22nd April, Camp III had been established on the threshold of the Western Cwm; now a route up it must be made, a site for Advance Base chosen.

In London, we had calculated that a period of about three weeks would be necessary for lifting our stores into the Western Cwm. The 'Build-up' plan was that this period should be divided into two halves, with a break for rest between them. During the first half, we should be mainly occupied with shifting loads from Base Camp to Camp III ('Low Level Ferry'); during the second, the centre of activity would be in the Western Cwm ('High Level Ferry' to Camp IV). To lift the loads, twenty-eight of our thirty-nine Sherpas would be required. They were to be divided into four parties; two members of the climbing party were to be assigned to each. I was most anxious that, in negotiating the known dangers of the Icefall and the expected hidden crevasses of the Cwm, the Sherpas should not be exposed to risks which were not shared by ourselves.

The task of entering and finding a route up to the head of the Western Cwm was undertaken by Charles Evans, Tenzing, Ed Hillary and myself. On the afternoon of 25th April, we started upwards from Camp III to have a preview of the prospects. We took with us three ladder sections, which we had estimated would be sufficient for bridging the narrowest gap of a big crevasse which had stopped Ed, George Band and I when we had prospected beyond the site of Camp III on 22nd April.

April 25th Putting the sections together, we lowered the ladder carefully across and crawled over one at a time. There remained many obstacles, as yet unseen, to getting up the Cwm, but somehow this moment when we stood together on the far side of that crevasse made a special impression on me. It symbolized our entry into the Cwm; we felt sure we were through.

In this elated mood we went on, late into the evening. One interesting passage, later known as 'Hunt's Gully', consisted of a very steep descent into the shallow depths of a crevasse, crossing the crack in the ice by a snow bridge and climbing out along the narrow terrace on the far side.

'Hunt's Gully'

Gradually we were able to work away towards the centre of the glacier. Its wrinkled surface smoothed out. As we went on we could see more and more up the Cwm: the whole of Lhotse, bathed in evening light, and then at last, still distant but dramatic, the South Col of Everest and the great slope below it. We turned back as the sun was setting behind Pumori and went down excitedly to our tents to tell the others.

This picture is typical of the lower part of the Cwm

April 26th   A brilliant morning. We were all in great spirits as we made our way into the Cwm, the reconnaissance party with Evans and myself leading on one rope, followed by Hillary and Tenzing. After them came Gregory and Noyce with their Sherpas, carrying the high priority stores for Advance Base and beyond.

Charles and I moved right-handed towards the south edge of the glacier, circumventing a 'step' or minor icefall some distance farther up. Planting flags as we went on, we rose up beside this 'step' and reached the upper part of the Cwm, smooth and stretching almost without break to a second 'step' guarding the foot of the slopes beneath the South Col and Lhotse – the distance might be one and a half miles.

In the Cwm; ferry party on the way to Camp IV

Hillary, Evans and Tenzing at the site of the Swiss Camp IV

After a three and a half hours' journey from Camp III, we reached the point where the Swiss had placed their Camp IV last autumn. Numerous containers were seen half-buried beneath the winter snow; their contents were exciting to surmise and no less satisfactory to discover. The weather had already closed in as we descended the Cwm that afternoon. The Ferry party had carried their loads to the top of the second 'step' and therefore done very well on this, their first trip up the Cwm.

The Ferry work went on day after day for nine days, running to an almost clockwork time-table. By 2nd May we had moved approximately ninety loads, each weighing an average of 40 lb., to Camp III, and, of these, about forty-five loads onwards to, or towards, our Advance Base, Camp IV. Our Ferry trains and their guards had well earned their rest.

71

Looking down the Cwm. Ferry parties

THE LHOTSE FACE

While the work of ferrying loads came to a temporary stop in the early days of May, an event of great significance was in progress: a reconnaissance of the Lhotse Face, the barrier which must be surmounted to arrive at the foot of the final pyramid. Our immediate objective was the saddle or depression between Lhotse and Everest: the South Col (26,000 feet). To reach it we must climb the steep slopes of ice and snow falling from the Col and Lhotse over a vertical distance of 4,000 feet. Not only would it be a strenuous and difficult undertaking to reach the Col; it would be necessary for considerable numbers of us to do so, carrying a large quantity of stores and equipment to enable the final assault to be launched with adequate support. One point stood out and was underlined by the hard experience of the Swiss: the absolute need to make at least one resting place in the eventual journey to the Col.

The most direct way to attain the Col is to force a crossing over the *Bergschrund* or horizontal crevasse skirting the foot of the Face and make for the Geneva Spur. But the slope is unrelentingly steep and much of it is ice-covered. There is virtually no natural resting-place for a tent between the Cwm and the Col, over a height of 4,000 feet. Only by discovering a route via the more devious Lhotse glacier could a camp site or sites be found and the ascent be made in stages.

This reconnaissance of the Lhotse Face was also a dress rehearsal for Everest, for experiments were to be carried out in the use of both Open and Closed-Circuit oxygen at higher altitudes than had been possible hitherto. The results of the reconnaissance and of the testing of the equipments would enable me to decide on the plans for the Assault.

'Bradley'
high altitude
boots

The model by Cockade L

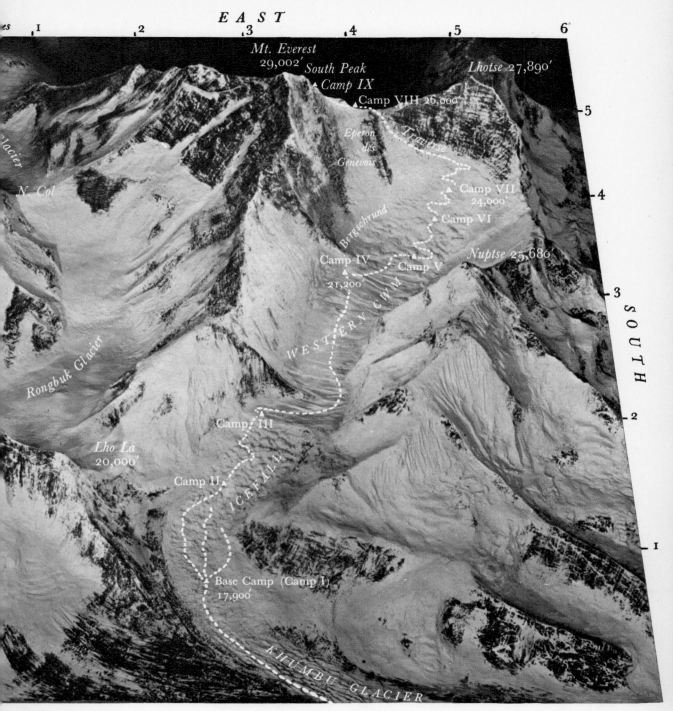

EAST

1   2   3   4   5   6

Mt. Everest
29,002' South Peak   Lhotse 27,890'
▲ Camp IX
▲ Camp VIII 26,000'   — 5

Eperon   Traverse
des
Genevois
▲ Camp VII
24,000'   — 4
Bergschrund   ▲ Camp VI

Camp IV ▲   ▲ Camp V   Nuptse 25,680'
21,200'   — 3

WESTERN CWM

N. Col

Rongbuk Glacier

Camp III ▲   — 2

Lho La   ICEFALL
20,000'

Camp II ▲   — 1

Base Camp (Camp I)
17,900'

KHUMBU GLACIER

…otographed from above

*Evans and Bourdillon are resting while breathing oxygen
from their closed-circuit sets. Hunt's oxygen set is in the foreground*

*An early picture of Camp IV
under the western
slopes of Everest*

May 1st Charles Evans, Tom Bourdillon and I went up the Cwm to establish Camp IV – so far it was no more than a dump of stores – on our way to get to grips with the Lhotse Face. We were to make a preliminary acquaintance of the Face next day and would then be joined by Wylie and Ward for the main reconnaissance. Next day we continued upwards, over untrodden ground. Above the second 'step' at the head of the Cwm, we found traces of the Swiss Camp V, at approximately 22,000 feet. One and a half hours after leaving this camp, we had climbed the first steep rise above the foot of the Lhotse Face. The traverse which we had seen from below started leftwards from this point and we rested for a while. The weather was now very bad. It seemed best to return rather than expend effort better reserved for the main reconnaissance.

75

Wylie directing the pitching of tents at Camp V. Above is the unclimbable South-west cliff of Everest

On May 4th the Reconnaissance party started up the Face in dismally bad weather. Casting more over to the left than we had done, they came upon the beginning of the Swiss autumn route. They struggled directly up it, then a short ice chimney led them by a zig-zag movement up and across some of the steepest ground yet encountered. As they went, they cleared a thick layer of loose, unreliable snow in order to cut ice steps. It was extremely exhausting. On a tiny shelf above were the tattered remains of the Swiss Camp VI. They struggled up to it, cleared a space and pitched their own tent. Wylie and his weary little party now plodded very slowly back to Camp V. Bourdillon and Evans remained, pushing up the Face to little short of 24,000 feet next day.

Camp VI

Before the South Col 'lift' could start, a route must be prepared at least as far as the Traverse from the head of the Lhotse glacier towards the Geneva Spur. This assignment I decided to give to George Lowe, a master of icecraft. On 11th May, George Lowe and four of our best Sherpas made their way up the Face under most difficult conditions to establish themselves at Camp VI. For the next few days, Lowe and Ang Nyima improved the track downwards towards Camp V, where Westmacott and the three other Sherpas were based, and also forced a route gradually upwards. On 14th May, in fine weather, they went up 1,000 feet and discovered the Swiss Camp VII.

The first tent of Camp VII

On 17th May, George and Wilfrid Noyce, who had replaced
Ang Nyima, not only established Camp VII on the Swiss site,
using gear carried up by Hillary on the 15th, but their delighted
spectators observed them in the afternoon emerging from
behind the sérac which conceals that camp and continuing
upwards for over 600 feet. The hopes of watchers below were
dashed when next morning Lowe, the newly-arrived Ward and
Da Tensing made a belated start only to turn back at a point
little higher than that reached before. The wind was so severe
they had done well to start out at all.

At Camp IV. Watching the Lhotse Face

May 19th   The drama of the Lhotse Face continued unabated. It was now the tenth day of the struggle. The wind continued to batter the west face of Everest high above us. We at Camp IV waited hour by hour that morning, vainly waiting for signs of movement. To increase our difficulties, we were no longer able to get any wireless communication with Camp VII. I was anxious to have a direct report from George Lowe himself on the situation up there. He must be tiring after his astonishing feat of endurance; Griff Pugh was even worried about the effect on the mind of so prolonged a period at over 23,000 feet.

Camp IV (Advance Base)

Life in Camp IV during those last few days before the Assault followed a regular pattern. At about eight o'clock in the morning, a cheery Sherpa face appears through the tent opening, with a mug of very sweet tea. You wait for the warmth of the sun to strike the tent roof; you come out into another Everest day. A quick glance upwards at the slopes of Lhotse: had they started out? No sign of movement there.

Breakfast in the big tent is a leisurely affair; we discuss the events of the day: an additional Sherpa for a Ferry team, a message for Base Camp, rations. Gradually most of us disperse till lunch, when everyone meets again in the Mess tent. Another look up at Camp VII: Tom Bourdillon and six Sherpas are seen crossing the last steep slope towards it with another 200 lb. of stores.

Thondup in his kitchen at Camp IV

The arrival of our head cook, Thondup, on the afternoon of the 18th with Tenzing, Wylie and the remainder of our tents and stores, was a joyous event. His presence at Advance Base – as we could now call Camp IV – would greatly raise morale. Food continued to be a subject of great interest to all of us.

At four o'clock there is tea, jam and biscuits, perhaps fruit cake. Then two parties are getting ready, shouldering

Sunset at Camp IV

loads, moving off up the track lying like a pencil line on the sun-glazed surface of the snow. At sunset Tom comes down with his party. 'The wind is terrific there,' is his comment on our enquiries regarding the progress of the Lhotse Face party that day. In the Mess tent we listen to the weather forecast for the expedition on the Overseas Service of the B.B.C. 'Overcast skies . . . heavy snow showers . . . wind.' This is a time for reading or writing, tucked warmly in a sleeping-bag, until someone shouts, 'Supper up.' Supper, some interesting conversation and discussion, and one more Everest day has slipped away. How long will it be before we are finished with this mountain?

Ward and Noyce at Camp VI

May 19th With Camp IV set up at full strength as Advance Base, I decided to fix the start for the South Col 'carry' next day, when the first party, led by Wilfrid Noyce, would go up to Camp V on the first stage of their journey. They would be followed on 20th May by Charles Wylie and a second team of Sherpas. Before leaving Wilfrid at Camp V on the evening of the 19th, I said: 'If George and Michael don't manage to prepare the Traverse before they come down tomorrow, you will have to decide at Camp VII whether to carry straight on with the Sherpas next day, or go up yourself first and prepare the track.'

Ang Nyima is fixing handlines on the Lhotse Face

George Lowe and Michael Ward did not give in easily. They made one more attempt to get up to the Traverse, but the long strain was telling greatly on their endurance. During those eleven days, George, supported at intervals by others, had put up a performance which will go down in the annals of mountaineering as an epic achievement of tenacity and skill.

The smaller picture shows a piton driven into the ice. The rope is attached to it by means of a snap-link or karabiner

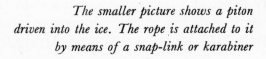

Camp VII with the Geneva Spur and the cliff of Everest beyond

May 21st   The morning dawned fine. We scanned the white expanse of snow above, hoping for an early start from Camp VII by the first 'carry'. Nothing happened till 10 a.m. Then two tiny dots emerged. Obviously Wilfrid had thought it necessary to go up himself first. Moreover, their progress was very slow. It was then I made up my mind to send up two climbers to reinforce the 'carry'. But everyone in the camp was either part of the first or second Assault teams, ready to start as soon as the 'carry' was completed, or resting after recent work on the Lhotse Face. The only solution was drastic: the lot must fall on Tenzing and Hillary, possibly to the detriment of their chances in the Assault. They willingly prepared themselves and left at mid-day.

Lhotse
27,890'

25,000'

24,000'

←VII

23,000'

VI

V

22,000'

George Lowe drew this map of the route up the Lhotse Face on to the photograph, taken at Camp IV. The morning light throws the glacier into relief, but Lowe's comment was that the picture gives no idea of steepness

Meanwhile we continued to watch the progress of Noyce and Annullu. At 12.30 they had passed the highest point reached so far and stood on the shelf beneath the final slopes sweeping up to Lhotse, where a traverse must be made to the left towards the couloir beside the Geneva Spur. Excitement mounted as we watched them move towards the famous Traverse, then the rocks of the Spur and beyond them, heading for the South Col itself.

Noyce above Camp VII

THE SOUTH COL

At 2.40 p.m. on the afternoon of 21st May, Wilfrid Noyce and his companion Annullu stood above the South Col of Everest, at about 26,000 feet. They were looking upwards to the final pyramid of Everest itself. It was a great moment for them both, and it was shared by all of us who watched them. Their presence there was symbolic of our success in overcoming the most crucial problem of the whole climb: they had reached an objective we had been striving to attain for twelve anxious days.

On the level plateau of the Col they found remains of the Swiss occupation.

They now returned to Camp VII, arriving there relatively fresh at 5.30 p.m. For Noyce 'it was one of the most enjoyable day's mountaineering I've ever had'.

Wylie, with a team of fourteen Sherpas, followed by Tenzing and Hillary, had now arrived at Camp VII. Noyce and Annullu were greeted with tremendous enthusiasm. The return of this pair, without distress or injury, after climbing

Everest, much foreshortened, and the top of the Geneva Spur seen from the traverse on the Lhotse Face. Below, at Camp IV, Pugh takes notes from Noyce and Wylie on their physical and mental reactions, after their return from the South Col. He will compare later accounts

steadily to the South Col that day, had made a profound impression on the waiting men. Morale rose suddenly, inspired by a fine example. If these two could do it, so could they. Spurred by Tenzing's encouragement and clear orders for the morrow, the success of the 'carry' was assured.

But the watchers in the Cwm could not know this. Our anxiety persisted the following morning as we again stared up the Lhotse Face, waiting for signs of activity at Camp VII.

Wylie's team of Sherpas on the lower part of the Lhotse Face

May 22nd   At 8.30 a.m., two little dots were seen coming out from behind the ice pinnacle at Camp VII. The Sherpas followed in a long string: seventeen, a seemingly incredible number at over 24,000 feet. The entire caravan was on its way, carrying our vital stores to the foot of the final peak. The Assault was on.

On 23rd May I left Camp V with the two Sherpas of the first Assault party, Da Namgyal and Ang Tensing. Tom Bourdillon and Charles Evans, who were to make the first of our two Assaults, followed us up to Camp VII.

Looking down into the Cwm from 25,000 feet on the Lhotse Face

The South Col from the top of the Geneva Spur. Everest hidden in cloud

May 24th We went up to the top of the Lhotse glacier very slowly, both ropes moving at a snail's pace. It was 4 p.m. when we topped the Geneva Spur. Above us, across the desolate plateau of the South Col, rose the South Peak of Everest, an elegant snow spire breathtakingly close, yet nearly 3,000 feet above our heads. It was a queer sensation to go down into the Col at the end of our long, hard climb – as though entering a trap.

Wind on the Col, May 24th. Behind Hunt is the wreckage of the Swiss Camp VI

The surface of this waste is partly covered by stones, partly with sheets of bare, bluish ice. The wind adds to the sense of dread which possesses this place. It was blowing fiercely as we went down the slope which must be descended from the top of the Spur to reach the Col. We were making towards the right where some patches of colour marked the remnants of the Swiss camp. There was little time to take stock of our surroundings; it was growing late and we must get our tents erected before the cold gripped us.

Camp VIII. On the South Col; 26,000 feet

We pulled out the Pyramid tent from the pile left by the South Col party on the 22nd and for over an hour fought and strove to put it up. Moving now without oxygen, we were far too weak to compete with the fiendish gale. But by about 5.30, it was up, more or less. The Meade tent for the two Sherpas took less time. By 9 p.m. we had brewed and drunk four mugfuls of liquid each; lemonade, soup, tea and cocoa. We eventually settled down for the night.

Tenzing and Hillary start from Advance Base, May 25th, for the second Assault

May 25th We felt refreshed next morning, the wind had relented, the weather was utterly clear. But we could not start. Food had to be sorted out; Ang Tensing was sick; the oxygen had not been prepared. Fortunately, from the viewpoint of the Assault programme, there was time. Ed Hillary's party would not arrive until the evening of next day. I tidied up around the tents, separating the Swiss gear from our own. Da Namgyal helped me to put up the third tent. I moved into it to leave Tom and Charles more space to prepare for their Assault next day.

THE SOUTH PEAK

To reach the top of Everest, the climber must set foot on and follow the South-East ridge which runs down from the summit to, or towards the South Col, passing on its way over the South Peak, 28,700 feet. The riddle on this final section was what lay beyond and between the two summits. It could not be seen from the Col, so the Swiss were unable to throw light on the problem.

The primary objective of the First Assault party – Tom Bourdillon and Charles Evans, using Closed-Circuit equipment – would be the South Peak. Only if the oxygen apparatus and supply were satisfactory, the weather fair and the terrain between the two peaks such as to allow them time to get there and back within safe limits should they attempt to go farther. This leading team would be followed immediately by Tenzing and Hillary, using Open-Circuit equipment.

I felt it necessary to have a supporting party close behind the first summit pair, particularly as we could not be sure that the interval between the two attempts might not become greater than twenty-four hours, due to bad weather or other causes. I had decided to attach myself, with two Sherpas, to the first pair, our very special responsibility being that of carrying the last camp up the South-East ridge to the highest possible point. I had in mind the Snow Shoulder, 28,000 feet. But when Ang Tensing fell sick at Camp VII, I decided the chances of Da Namgyal and myself carrying our share of the loads required for the top camp to the Shoulder were very small. It seemed best now to take the loads as high as we could, leaving the second support party, who had rather less to lift, the task of taking them on. Gregory and three Sherpas were to be in support of Hillary and Tenzing; in the event, Lowe joined their party.

Da Namgyal and I started off towards the South-East ridge soon after 7 a.m., each carrying about 45 lb. and using oxygen. We moved very slowly. After about half an hour, I was delighted to see Bourdillon and Evans coming up fast from behind; they must have put right the defect in their oxygen apparatus which had delayed them. It was not until twenty-four hours later that I found my own set had been ice-blocked, a possible explanation of the extraordinary difficulty I experienced in breathing and climbing that day. As Da Namgyal and I stopped to take our first rest, Tom and Charles went ahead up the snow-filled couloir. Our progress grew more exhausting, but the ridge was now close. About 300 feet below the Snow Shoulder, Da Namgyal said he could do no more; I was near enough my own limit. We left our loads at 27,350 feet and descended slowly with extreme precaution. Tenzing and Hillary helped us to the tents.

Evans and Bourdillon

The dump of stores left by Hunt and Da Namgyal at 27,350 feet

May 26th   Tom Bourdillon and Charles Evans reached 27,200 feet on the South-East ridge shortly after 9 a.m. But from this point onwards the going became worse. In two hours, indeed, they had not covered half the distance towards the South Peak. They paused at the Snow Shoulder, changed their canisters, leaving the others one-third full, and went on. They arrived at the foot of the final steep rise, a great slope tilting abruptly at a high angle. On and on, up those last 400 feet, very slowly now. Then quite suddenly the angle eased, and almost at once they found themselves upon the South Peak of Everest, at 28,200 feet.

Bourdillon photographed by Evans on the South Summit, looking at the final ridge

Through a gap in the clouds Bourdillon took this photograph of the Kangshung Glacier, to the east

It was 1 o'clock. Should they go on? For them here was a unique opportunity to climb to the top. But Charles reckoned it might take them three hours to reach it, another two hours back to the South Peak. They would long since have exhausted their supply of oxygen and at 6 p.m. would have nearly 3,000 feet to descend to safety. In fact, it was out of the question. Reluctantly they turned to go down.

At 3.30 there was a thinning of the cloud above the couloir and we saw them there.

Evans and Bourdillon returning, coming towards Camp VIII from the foot of the Couloir

At 4.30 they approached the tents and we went out to meet them, burdened with their cumbersome equipment and bulky clothing, their faces frost-covered, looking like strangers from another planet. Both were utterly weary. It was natural that disappointment should have been among their feelings, yet they had achieved exactly what had been hoped of them. Their feat in climbing to over 28,700 feet and back in one day was a magnificent effort, and a triumph also for the oxygen equipment on which such infinite pains had been taken. They had sighted that last part of the ridge and were able to describe it to Tenzing and Hillary. They had given us all incalculable confidence in final victory.

We were overcrowded that evening at Camp VIII. The Pyramid tent was occupied by the second Assault party, Hillary, Tenzing, Gregory and Lowe, while we of the first party occupied the Meade, designed for two. The three Sherpas of the second support team – Ang Nyima, Pemba and Ang Temba – somehow managed to squeeze into the tiny 'Blister' tent. It was a terrible night. Continually buffeted by the gale, there was no question of sleep.

Tenzing and Lowe at Camp VIII

May 27th My diary for this day reads as follows:

'It was no surprise to find at about 8 a.m. that Ed Hillary's party had not started. The wind was blowing like mad. Of the Sherpas, only Ang Nyima was showing any sign of life. A postponement of the Assault for twenty-four hours was imperative; fortunately we have stock-piled enough to make this possible.

'At about midday Charles and Tom started off on their way down. Then Charles suddenly re-appeared with the alarming news that Tom was in a critical state. Another of us must accompany him down. I decided I must go. Left Ed with parting instructions not to give in if avoidable and promising to send up a reinforcement party.'

A clear day on the South Col. Tenzing beside the Pyramid tent

As we staggered down the last few feet to Camp VII, to our relief and delight we were met by Wilf Noyce and Mike Ward, who helped us in and prepared our supper. Wilfrid's presence at Camp VII was very fortunate. He was halfway to the Col and, unbeknown to him, I had told Ed Hillary I would send him up with three more volunteer Sherpas with further stores. Charles Evans found energy to continue down to Advance Base the same evening to arrange for three men to come up and join Noyce at Camp VII next day.

On the morning of 28th May, as Tom and I descended to the Cwm, we met Charles Wylie with three Sherpas on their way up with replenishments. We reached Advance Base in the early afternoon. There was nothing for us now to do but await the outcome of the second Assault.

Pasang Dawa, Dawa Thondup, Ang Norbu, Pasang Phutar, Topkie, Annullu.
These Sherpas twice carried loads to the South Col without oxygen

The Sherpas were magnificent, their co-operation beyond praise. Of our total team of twenty-seven Sherpas chosen for the work above the Western Cwm, nineteen men went to the South Col, six of them twice. In terms of stores, this means we lifted some 750 lb. up to 26,000 feet; this it was that enabled our Assault teams to remain there in good spirits and without suffering undue deterioration over a longer period than had been expected.

THE SUMMIT _by Edmund Hillary_

Early on the morning of 27th May I awoke from an uneasy sleep feeling very cold and miserable. My companions in our Pyramid tent, Lowe, Gregory and Tenzing, were all tossing and turning in unsuccessful efforts to gain relief from the bitter cold. The relentless wind was blowing in all its fury. Reluctantly removing my hand from my sleeping bag I looked at my watch. It was 4 a.m. In the flickering light of a match, the thermometer lying against the tent wall read – 25 Centigrade.

We had hoped to establish a camp high on the South-East ridge that day, but the force of the wind obviously made a start impossible. At 9 a.m. the wind was still blowing fiercely, and clad in all my warm clothing I crawled out of the tent and crossed to the small Meade tent housing John Hunt, Charles Evans and Tom Bourdillon. Ang Temba had become sick and was obviously incapable of carrying up any farther. So we decided to send him down with Evans and Bourdillon when they left for Camp VII at about midday. Hunt decided at the last moment to accompany this party, owing to Bourdillon's condition, and George Lowe and I assisted a very weary foursome to climb the slopes above the camp and then watched them start off on their slow and exhausting trip down to Camp VII.

All day the wind blew furiously and it was in a somewhat desperate spirit that we organized the loads for the establishment of the Ridge Camp the following day. The violent wind gave us another unpleasant night, but we were all breathing oxygen and this enabled us to doze uneasily for seven or eight hours.

Early next morning the wind was still blowing strongly, but about 8 a.m. it eased considerably and we decided to leave. Pemba had been violently ill all night; only one Sherpa porter, Ang Nyima, was left to carry for us out of our original band of three. Our only alternative was to carry the camp ourselves. We repacked the loads, having no choice but to cut down vital supplies of oxygen.

At 8.45 a.m. Lowe, Gregory and Ang Nyima departed, all carrying over 40 lb. each and breathing oxygen at 5 litres a minute. Tenzing and I were to leave later so that we could follow quickly up the steps they had made and so conserve energy and oxygen. We set off at 10 a.m. carrying 50 lb. apiece.

South Peak

Camp IX 27,900'

Dump of Stores 27,350'

Swiss Camp VII

Couloir

S O U T H C O L

25,850'

Hillary's clothing and equipment on May 29th

A skullcap on to which clipped the oxygen mask. A down hood attached to the down jacket. A windproof hood attached to the windproof jacket and done up under the chin. Snowglasses (aluminium frames, no side shields).

A string singlet. A short-sleeved woollen vest. A long-sleeved Shetland pullover. A woollen tartan shirt (New Zealand type). A down jacket zipped up to the neck, with elastic cuffs. A windproof jacket zipped up to the neck. A thin nylon line wound six times round his waist, threaded through the metal clip or "Karabiner" onto which the nylon rope itself was tied.

Short cellular underpants. Long woollen underpants. Down trousers with elastic ankles. Windproof trousers with elastic strap under the instep.

Two pairs woollen socks. High altitude boots.

Three pairs of gloves: silk, woollen, windproof.

The open-circuit oxygen equipment with one bottle of oxygen only in the middle frame.

His ice-axe.

In a wide zip pocket the full width of the front of the windproof jacket at chest level: His camera with the lens hood (which included an ultra-violet filter which he put on for each photograph taken on the summit). The leather strap of the camera was round his neck. His spares (gloves, etc.). A few English coins which just happened to be there.

Gregory and Ang Nyima at the head of the Couloir

We followed slowly up the long slopes to the foot of the great couloir and then climbed the veritable staircase hewn by Lowe in the firm steep snow of the couloir. As we moved slowly up the steps we were bombarded by a constant stream of ice chips falling from well above us where Lowe and Gregory were cutting steps across to the South-East ridge. We reached the ridge at midday and joined the other party.

Nearby was the tattered ruin of the Swiss tent of the previous spring, and it added an air of loneliness and desolation to this remarkable viewpoint. From here Lambert and Tenzing had made their gallant attempt to reach the summit after a night spent without sleeping bags. It was a wonderful spot with tremendous views in every direction, and we indulged in an orgy of photography.

Hillary and Tenzing in the Couloir. Behind them, two miles away, is the Lhotse Face

We were all feeling extremely well and felt confident of placing our camp high up on the South-East ridge. We heaved on our loads again and moved 150 feet up the ridge to the dump made by Hunt two days previously. The dump was at 27,350 feet, but we considered this was still far too low for an effective summit camp, so somewhat reluctantly we added all this extra gear to our already large loads. We continued up the ridge at a somewhat reduced rate, moving steadily, though slowly.

The remains of the Swiss Camp VII at 27,200 feet

Hillary and Tenzing at 27,200 feet

The ridge steepened on to a slope of firm snow and Lowe chipped steps up it for fifty feet. By 2 p.m. we were beginning to tire and started looking for a camp site. The ridge continued upwards in one unbroken sweep. We plugged slowly on, looking for a ledge without success. We were getting a little desperate until Tenzing, remembering the ground from the previous year, suggested a traverse over steep slopes to the left, which finally landed us on to a relatively flat spot beneath a rock bluff. It was 2.30 and we decided to camp here. We estimated our height at 27,900 feet.

Lowe, Gregory and Ang Nyima dropped their loads on to the site with relief. They were tired but well satisfied with the height gained. Wasting no time, they hurried off back to the South Col.

Approaching 28,000 feet, at the site of Camp IX

West Shoulder

—Camp IX 28,000 ft.

It was with a certain feeling of loneliness that we watched our cheerful companions slowly descending the ridge, but we had much to do. We set to work with our ice-axes to clear the tiny platform and scratched off all the snow to reveal a rock slope at an angle of some 30 degrees. We pitched our tent on its double level and tied it down as best we could. While Tenzing began heating some soup, I made a tally of our limited oxygen supplies. For the Assault we had only one and two-third bottles each. I estimated that if we reduced our supplies to three litres per minute we might still have a chance.

As the sun set we crawled finally into our tent, put on all our warm clothing and wriggled into our sleeping-bags. We drank vast quantities of liquid and had a satisfying meal out of our store of delicacies: sardines on biscuits, tinned apricots, dates and jam and honey. We had sufficient oxygen for only four hours' sleep at one litre per minute. I decided to use this in two periods of two hours.

At 4 a.m. it was very still. I opened the tent door and looked far out across the dark and sleeping valleys of Nepal. The icy peaks below us were glowing clearly. We started up our cooker and to prevent the weaknesses arising from dehydration drank large quantities of lemon juice and sugar and followed this with our last tin of sardines on biscuits. I dragged our oxygen sets into the tent, completely rechecked and tested them. Over our down clothing we donned our windproofs and on to our hands we pulled three pairs of gloves.

At 6.30 a.m. we crawled out of our tent into the snow, hoisted our 30 lb. of oxygen gear on to our backs, connected up our masks and turned on the valves to bring life-giving oxygen into our lungs. A few good deep breaths and we were ready to go. The ridge was now all bathed in sunlight and we could see our first objective, the South Peak, far above us. We reached it at 9 a.m. The virgin ridge ahead was certainly impressive, even rather frightening.

The summit ridge of Everest. When this picture was taken by Hillary four men had seen the ridge; none had set foot on it

The 40-ft step

The South Peak (right) and part of the summit ridge. The snow cornices hang over a sheer drop of 10,000 feet

We cut a seat for ourselves just below the South Peak and removed our oxygen. Once again I worked out the mental arithmetic that was one of my main preoccupations on the way up and down the mountain. As our first partly full bottle of oxygen was now exhausted, we had only one full bottle left. Eight hundred litres of oxygen at three litres a minute? How long could we last? I estimated that this should give us $4\frac{1}{2}$ hours of going. Our apparatus was now much lighter and as I cut steps down off the South Summit I felt a distinct sense of freedom and well-being quite contrary to what I had expected at this great altitude.

As my ice-axe bit into the first steep slope of the ridge, my highest hopes were realized. The snow was crystalline and firm. We moved one at a time. I realized that our margin of safety at this altitude was not great and that we must take every care and precaution. I would cut a forty-foot line of steps, Tenzing belaying me while I worked. Then in turn I would sink the shaft of my ice-axe and put a few loops of rope round it and Tenzing, protected against a breaking step, would move up to me. Then once again I would go on cutting.

After an hour's steady going we reached the foot of the most formidable looking problem on the ridge – a rock step some forty feet high. We realized that at this altitude it might well spell the difference between success and failure. The rock itself, smooth and almost holdless, was here a barrier beyond our feeble strength to overcome. Fortunately, another possibility of tackling it still remained: a narrow crack running up the full forty feet of the step. I jammed my way into this crack. Taking advantage of every little rock hold and all the force I could muster, I literally cramponed backwards up the crack.

As Tenzing paid out the rope I inched my way upwards until I finally dragged myself out of the crack on to a wide ledge. For a few moments I lay regaining my breath and for the first time felt the fierce determination that nothing now could stop us reaching the top. As I heaved hard on the rope Tenzing wriggled his way up the crack and collapsed at the top like a giant fish just hauled from the sea.

I checked both our oxygen sets and roughly calculated our flow rates. Everything seemed to be going well. Tenzing's only comment when I enquired of his condition was to smile and wave along the ridge. It continued as before. I went on cutting steps on the narrow strip of snow. The ridge seemed never-ending. Our original zest had now quite gone and it was turning more into a grim struggle. I then realized that the ridge ahead, instead of still monotonously rising, now dropped sharply away, and far below I could see the South Col and the Rongbuk Glacier. I looked upwards to see a narrow snow ridge running up to a snowy summit. A few more whacks of the ice-axe in the firm snow and we stood on top.

My initial feelings were of relief – relief that there were no more steps to cut, no more ridges to traverse and no more humps to tantalize us with hopes of success. I looked at Tenzing and in spite of the balaclava, goggles and oxygen mask that concealed his face, there was no disguising his infectious grin of pure delight. It was 11.30 a.m. The ridge had taken us two and a half hours, but it seemed like a lifetime.

We shook hands and then Tenzing threw his arms round my shoulders and we thumped each other on the back until we were almost breathless. I turned off the oxygen and removed my set. I had carried my camera, loaded with colour film, inside my shirt to keep

FROM THE SUMMIT, LOOKING EAST

it warm, so I now produced it and got Tenzing to pose for me on the top, waving his ice-axe on which was a string of flags – British, Nepalese, United Nations and Indian. Then I turned my attention to the great stretch of country lying below us. To the east was our giant neighbour Makalu, unexplored and unclimbed. Far away across the clouds the great bulk of Kangchenjunga loomed on the horizon. To the west, Cho Oyu, dominated the scene. The most important photograph, I felt, was a shot down the North Ridge showing the route made famous by those great climbers of the 1920s and 1930s.

Meanwhile, Tenzing had made a little hole in the snow and in it he placed various articles of food. Small offerings, indeed, but at least a token gift to the Gods all devout Buddhists believe have their home on this lofty summit. Two days before, Hunt had given me a small crucifix which he asked me to take to the top. I placed it beside Tenzing's gifts.

Lhotse II   Lhotse I   Hongu Glacier

SOUTH

Pumori   *Cho Oyu*   *Gyachung Kang*

Lingtren   *West Rongb*
Glaci

W E S T

– Lho La

On pages 117-121
all the summit
photographs are
reproduced.
On this and the
preceding page,
pairs of pictures
have been joined
together.

*buk
cier*

*North
Col*

N O R T H

After fifteen minutes we turned to go. We would have to move fast in order to reach the life-saving reserve of two oxygen bottles left below the South Summit by Bourdillon and Evans. We both felt a little tired; we must get off the mountain quickly. Spurred by the urgency of diminishing oxygen, we cramponed along our tracks. In what seemed almost miraculous time, we reached the top of the rock step, kicked and jammed our way down it again. We scrambled cautiously over the rock traverse and back to the South Peak. Only one hour from the top! As I led down the great snow slope, I packed each step as carefully as if our lives depended on it, as well they might. We were now very tired but moved automatically down to the two reserve cylinders on the ridge. As we were only a short distance from the camp and had a few litres of oxygen left in our own bottles, we carried the extra cylinders down our tracks and reached our tent on its crazy platform at 2 p.m. Tenzing made a lemonade drink, heavily sweetened; I changed our oxygen sets on to the last partly-filled bottles. We turned downwards with dragging feet.

Our faculties seemed numbed and time passed as in a dream. As we cramponed wearily down the long slopes above the South Col, two figures came towards us and met us a few hundred feet above the camp. They were Lowe and Noyce, laden with hot soup and emergency oxygen. We were too tired to make any response to Lowe's enthusiastic acceptance of our news. Just short of the tents my oxygen ran out. We had had enough to do the job, but by no means too much. We crawled into the tent and with a sigh of sheer delight collapsed into our sleeping bags.

Early the following morning we made slow but determined preparations for our departure. As we came down the ice steps towards Camp VII our main wish was to rest. The hot drinks which Wylie and the Sherpas pressed into our hands and their joyful acceptance of our news were a great stimulant. We went on down the Lhotse glacier mentally if not physically refreshed.

Fifty yards from Camp IV, Lowe gave the 'thumbs up' signal and waved his ice-axe in the direction of the summit. Immediately the scene was galvanized into activity and our approaching companions ran towards us. To see the unashamed joy spread over the tired, strained face of our gallant and determined leader was to me reward enough.

This photograph was taken at 12.45 p.m. on 29th May 1953. It shows the footmarks of Tenzing and Hillary coming down the left of the ridge

Tenzing coming down the Lhotse Face

May 30th　This was IT: Hillary and Tenzing had made it! Everyone was pouring out of the tents: there were shouts of joy. Amid much chatter we escorted them into camp. We all went into the Mess tent to hear the great story. Devouring an omelette, draining mugfuls of his favourite lemonade drink, Ed Hillary told it in graphic yet simple terms, while James Morris scribbled notes for his message to the world. That evening I looked around the tent at these men who had finished the job, all of them now relaxed, happy, exuberant. How fully each and all had shared in the achievement so brilliantly concluded by Tenzing and Hillary! I felt an immense pride in these companions of mine.

125

June 2nd All were gathered at Base Camp by this afternoon, after much good work on a reverse Ferry service to bring back our gear. In our Mess tent after supper we turned on the wireless to hear the Coronation news. In the second headline of the summary, the announcer said: 'The wonderful news broke in London last night that Everest has been climbed by the British expedition. . . .' We were dumbfounded. Before leaving us in the Cwm, James Morris had said he hoped to get a brief message back quickly, but none of us had imagined it could already have been known at home twenty-four hours ago. With growing excitement we listened further. The Queen and the Prime Minister had sent telegrams of congratulation to us; the news had been announced over the loudspeakers along the Coronation route; the crowds had cheered. It all sounded like a fairy tale.

What were the reasons for our success? To these factors the triumph should be attributed, it matters not in what proportion: to all who had climbed on Everest before; to our planning and other preparations; to the excellence of our equipment; to our Sherpas and ourselves; to the favour of the elements. And I would add one more factor, less easy to assess: the thoughts and prayers of all those who watched and waited and hoped for our success.

Was it worth while? For us who took part in the venture, it was so beyond doubt. We have shared a high endeavour; we have witnessed scenes of beauty and grandeur; we have built up a lasting comradeship among ourselves and we have seen the fruits of that comradeship ripen into achievement. We shall not forget those moments of great living upon that mountain.